JOHN MUIR

PEOPLE WHO MADE A DIFFERENCE

David and Patricia Armentrout

Rourke Publishing LLC
Vero Beach, Florida 32964

PHOTO CREDITS:
©PhotoDisc, Inc.
©Library of Congress

EDITORIAL SERVICES:
Pamela Schroeder

Library of Congress Cataloging-in-Publication Data

Armentrout, David, 1962-
  John Muir / David & Patricia Armentrout
    p. cm. — (People who made a difference)
  ISBN 1-58952-055-6
  1. Muir, John, 1838-1914—Juvenile literature. 2. Naturalists—United
States—Biography—Juvenile literature. 3. Conservationists—United
States—Biography—Juvenile literature. [1. Muir, John, 1838-1914. 2. Naturalists. 3.
Conservationists.] I. Armentrout, Patricia, 1960- II. Title.

QH31.M9 A84 2001
333.7'2'092—dc21
[B]   2001018585

Printed in the USA

TABLE OF CONTENTS

JOHN MUIR

John Muir was born in Scotland in 1838. When John was ten his father moved the family to America.

John spent his boyhood working on the family farm. He did not go to school but he would read books on his own.

John's favorite thing to do was explore the wild lands around his home. He loved to hike in the forests and look at the plants and animals.

John Muir loved the outdoors more than anything.

JOHN THE INVENTOR

John read a lot about machines. He invented some, too. At age 22, John left the farm and took some of his inventions to a fair in Madison. John won money for his work.

John stayed in Madison and went to the university there. **Botany** was one subject John really enjoyed.

John with his good friend and writer John Burroughs

JOHN'S GREATEST LOVE

John worked on machines to earn money, but his greatest love was wandering through the wilderness.

In 1867 John took a **compass**, some maps, and very little else, and walked about 25 miles (40 km) a day. John's long trip took him to Florida, Cuba, then on a boat to New York. John then sailed to San Francisco, California. He wanted to see the **Yosemite** Valley.

John needed very little to be comfortable in the wilderness.

YOSEMITE VALLEY

The Yosemite Valley area is in the **Sierra Nevada** Mountains. John was amazed by the beauty of the valley. It was so different from the other places John had visited.

John wondered how the valley was made. He thought **glaciers** had cut and carved the valley. John pounded stakes in the ice-covered mountains. Over time, he measured how the ice moved. He proved that glaciers made the Yosemite Valley.

John Muir proved that glaciers carved the Yosemite Valley.

YEARS OF WANDERING

For years John explored the wilderness. He wrote articles about what he had learned in the wild lands.

John wandered hundreds of miles in the Yosemite Valley and in the **sequoia** region of California. He went to Lake **Tahoe**, and then north to climb Mount Shasta.

In 1876, John wrote an article about forest **conservation**. He wanted everyone to know how important is was to save America's wilderness areas.

Mount Shasta is in northern California.

GLACIER BAY, ALASKA

In 1879 John traveled to Alaska. He climbed and studied glaciers. One glacier now bears his name.

John went back to California that fall. He planned a wedding with Louie Strentzel. John and Louie married in 1880. They had two daughters by 1886.

Louie knew that John needed time in the wilderness. While John explored, Louie spent time reading, gardening, and enjoying John's letters and drawings.

John Muir traveled to Alaska to study glaciers and discovered Glacier Bay.

NATIONAL PARK SYSTEM

John was afraid that some day Yosemite Valley would be destroyed. He wrote articles to warn people about destroying the forests. This led to the creation of Yosemite National Park in 1890. John Muir is called the "Father of Our National Park System."

Two years later John and his friends formed the Sierra Club. The Sierra Club works to preserve American wilderness and wildlife.

MEETING PRESIDENT ROOSEVELT

John traveled all over the world studying forests. However, he always came back to the Sierra Nevada.

John met President Roosevelt in Yosemite Valley in 1903. They camped together. They talked about ways to save America's wild lands.

John spent his last years writing and spending time in Yosemite. He died in 1914 at the age of 76. John Muir is remembered as America's most famous conservationist.

President Theodore Roosevelt visited John Muir in Yosemite Valley.

JOHN MUIR'S LEGACY

You can understand John Muir's love of nature when visiting some of his favorite places. Many places have John's name. Muir Woods National Monument is near San Francisco. There you can walk trails lined with huge redwood trees. John Muir's home near San Francisco is a National Historic site. Of course, Muir Glacier can be seen in Alaska's Glacier Bay National Park.

John farmed with his father-in-law Dr. John Strentzel, shown here on his California farm.

IMPORTANT DATES TO REMEMBER

1838	Born in Dunbar, Scotland (April 21)
1849	Muir family sails to America.
1860	Wins prize money for his inventions
1868	Sails to San Francisco, California
1870	Proves Glacier Theory
1879	Discovers Glacier Bay, Alaska
1880	Marries Louie Strentzel
1890	Yosemite becomes National Park
1892	Forms the Sierra Club
1914	Dies in Los Angeles (December 24)

GLOSSARY

botany (BAHT eh nee) — a kind of science that deals with plants and plant life

compass (KAHM pes) — a tool used to find direction, like north, south, east, and west

conservation (KAHN ser VAY shen) — saving and managing natural resources, like forests

glaciers (GLAY sherz) — large bodies of ice that move slowly down a slope or valley

sequoia (si KWOUI eh) — a huge coniferous, or evergreen, redwood tree in California

Sierra Nevada (see AIR eh ne VAD eh) — mountain range in California

Tahoe (TAH hoh) — a large freshwater lake on the border of California and Nevada

Yosemite (yoe SEM ih tee) — a wilderness preserve in California named after the Yosemite Indians that used to live there

INDEX

Further Reading

Fox, Stephen R. *John Muir and His Legacy*. Little Brown & Company, Canada ©1981

Green, Carol. *John Muir Man of the Wild Places*. Children's Press, Chicago ©1991

Wadsworth, Ginger. *John Muir Wilderness Protector.* Lerner Publications,
   Minneapolis ©1992

Websites To Visit

•www.sierraclub.org/history/muir

About The Authors

David and Patricia Armentrout specialize in nonfiction writing. They have had several books published for primary school reading. They reside in Cincinnati, Ohio with their two children.